ÆSOP'S FABLES

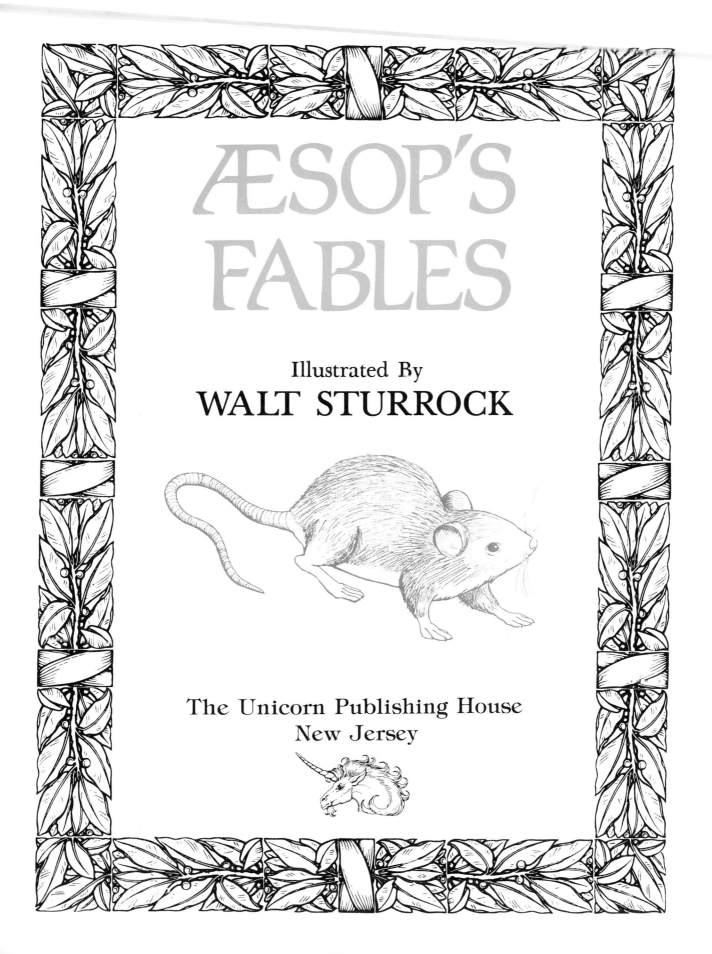

ÆSOP'S FABLES

Illustrated By
WALT STURROCK

The Unicorn Publishing House
New Jersey

Designed and edited by Jean L. Scrocco
Associate Juvenile Editor: Heidi K.L. Corso
Printed in Singapore by Singapore National Printers Ltd through Palace Press
Typography by Straight Creek Company, Denver, CO
Reproduction Photography by The Color Wheel, New York, NY

♦ ♦ ♦ ♦ ♦

♦ ♦ ♦ ♦ ♦

Distributed in Canada by Doubleday Canada, Ltd., Toronto, ON M5B 1Y3, Canada

♦ ♦ ♦ ♦ ♦

Special thanks to the entire Unicorn staff

♦ ♦ ♦ ♦ ♦

Printing History 15   14   13   12   11   10   9   8   7   6   5   4   3   2   1

Library of Congress Cataloging-in-Publication Data

Aesop's fables.
Aesop's fables / edited by Jean L. Scrocco; illustrated by Walt Sturrock.
p.   cm.
Summary: Thirty fables of Aesop, including "The Hare and the Tortoise," "The Ant and the Grasshopper," and "Androcles and the Lion."
ISBN O-88101-086-3: $14.95
1. Fables. [1. Fables.]   I. Scrocco, Jean L., 1952-   II. Sturrock, Walt, 1961- ill.   III. Title.
PZ8.2.A254   1988   88-10658
398.2 '452--dc19   CIP
[E]   AC

Additional Classic and Contemporary Editions
Richly Illustrated in
This Unicorn Heirloom Collection:

PHANTOM OF THE OPERA
DAVY AND THE GOBLIN
POLLYANNA
TWENTY THOUSAND LEAGUES UNDER THE SEAS
PETER PAN
ANTIQUE FAIRY TALES
PINOCCHIO
POE
THE WIZARD OF OZ
DRACULA
HEIDI
FROM TOLKIEN TO OZ
PETER COTTONTAIL'S SURPRISE
A CHRISTMAS TREASURY
TREASURES OF CHANUKAH

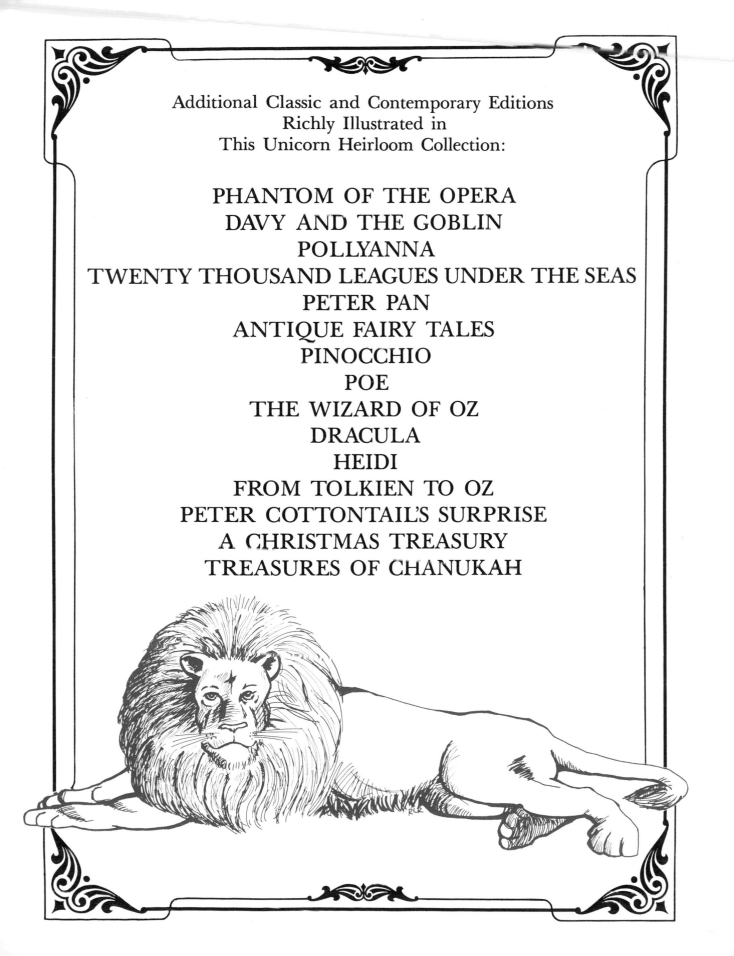

This edition of
AESOP'S FABLES
is dedicated to
Elizabeth A. Holmes
for her love, patience,
understanding, and hard work.

Walt Sturrock

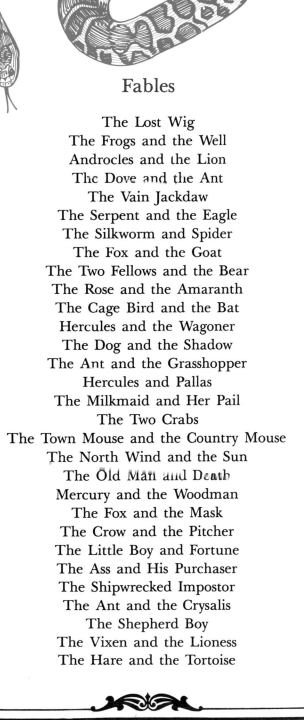

Fables

A very special thanks to my friends and family, who posed for the characters in this edition of *Aesop's Fables*. Their time and love enabled me to tame the animals of Aesop and honor his Gods.

CAST OF CHARACTERS

David Sturrock—Town Mouse
Tracy Petrillo—Country Mouse
Ted Fattoross—Ant; Grasshopper; North Wind; Purchaser
Elizabeth Holmes—Hare; The Rose; Lioness
Henrietta—Tortoise
Louise Mondello, Jr.—Androcles
Clifford O. Holmes, Jr.—Emperor
Lyman M. Dally—Hercules; Mercury; Zeus
Walter R. Sturrock—Wagoner
Ernest C. Hofer—Sun
Robert Vincent, Jr.—Shepherd Boy; Little Boy
Muffin—Dog with Meat
Alexander T. Kojak—Zeus
Cyndi Monahan—Milkmaid
Doug Corriston—Countryman; Fellow Playing Dead
Ted Guerin—Old Man
Barbara Sturrock—Death
Frank Foley—Traveler; Fellow in Tree; Lion; Puma
Ruth Williams—Fortune; Pallas
Bonnie Corriston—Vixen
Lori Sanders—Tiger
Robert Vincent, Sr.—Woodsman

Henrietta the Tortoise and Muffin the dog compliments of Elizabeth A. Holmes

LIST OF ILLUSTRATIONS

ÆSOP'S FABLES

THE LOST WIG

funny old lion, who had the misfortune to lose his mane, was wearing a wig as he was taking a stroll on a very windy day.

Looking up, he spied one of the charming Tiger sisters across the street, and, wishing to make an impression, smiled blandly and made a beautiful low bow. At that moment a very smart gust of wind came up, and the consequence was that his wig flew off and left him there, feeling foolish and looking worse, with his bald head glistening like a billiard ball. Though somewhat embarrassed at first, he smiled at the Lady and said: "Is it a wonder that another fellow's hair shouldn't keep on my head, when my own wouldn't stay there?"

Wit always has an answer ready.

THE FROGS AND THE WELL

wo Frogs lived together in a marsh. But one hot summer the marsh dried up, and they left it to look for another place to live in: for frogs like damp places if they can get them. By and by they came to a deep well, and one of them looked down into it, and said to the other, "This looks a nice cool place. Let us jump in and settle here." But the other, who had a wiser head on his shoulders, replied, "Not so fast, my friend. Supposing this well dried up like the marsh, how should we get out again?"

Look before you leap.

ANDROCLES AND THE LION

A slave named Androcles once escaped from his master and fled to the forest. As he was wandering about there he came upon a Lion lying down moaning and groaning. At first he turned to flee, but finding that the Lion did not pursue him, he turned back and went up to him. As he came near, the Lion put out his paw, which was all swollen and bleeding, and Androcles found that a huge thorn had got into it, and was causing all the pain. He pulled out the thorn and bound up the paw of the Lion, who was soon able to rise and lick the hand of Androcles like a dog. Then the Lion took Androcles to his cave, and every day used to bring him meat from which to live. But shortly afterwards both Androcles and the Lion were captured, and the slave was sentenced to be thrown to the Lion, after the latter had been kept without food for several days. The Emperor and all his Court came to see the spectacle, and Androcles was led out into the middle of the arena. Soon the Lion was let loose from his den, and rushed bounding and roaring towards his victim. But as soon as he came near to Androcles he recognized his friend, and fawned upon him, and licked his hands like a friendly dog. The Emperor, surprised at this, summoned Androcles to him, who told him the whole story. Whereupon the slave was pardoned and freed, and the Lion let loose to his native forest.

Gratitude is the sign of noble souls.

THE DOVE AND THE ANT

n Ant, going to a river to drink, fell in, and was carried along in the stream. A Dove pitied her condition, and threw into the the river a small bough, by means of which the Ant gained the shore. The Ant afterward, seeing a man with a fowling-piece aiming at the Dove, stung him in the foot sharply, and made him miss his aim, and so saved the Dove's life.

Little friends may prove great friends.

THE VAIN JACKDAW

upiter announced that he intended to appoint a king over the birds, and named a day on which they were to appear before his throne, when he would select the most beautiful of them all to be their ruler. Wishing to look their best on the occasion they repaired to the banks of a stream, where they busied themselves in washing and preening their feathers. The Jackdaw was there along with the rest, and realized that, with his ugly plumage, he would have no chance of being chosen as he was: so he waited till they were all gone, and then picked up the most gaudy of the feathers they had dropped, and fastened them about his own body, with the result that he looked gayer than any of them. When the appointed day came, the birds assembled before Jupiter's throne. After passing them in review, he was about to make the Jackdaw king, when all the rest set upon the king-select, stripped him of his borrowed plumes, and exposed him for the Jackdaw that he was.

It is not only fine feathers
that make fine birds.

THE SERPENT AND THE EAGLE

n Eagle swooped down upon a Serpent and seized it in his talons with the intention of carrying it off and devouring it. But the Serpent was too quick for him and had its coils round him in a moment; and then there ensued a life-and-death struggle between the two. A countryman, who was a witness of the encounter, came to the assistance of the eagle, and succeeded in freeing him from the Serpent and enabling him to escape. In revenge, the Serpent spat some of his poison into the man's drinking-horn. Heated with his exertions, the man was about to slake his thirst with a draught from the horn, when the Eagle knocked it out of his hand, and spilled its contents upon the ground.

One good turn deserves another.

THE SILKWORM AND SPIDER

aving received an order for twenty yards of silk from Princess Lioness, the Silkworm sat down at her loom and worked away with zeal. A Spider soon came around and asked to hire a web-room near by. The Silkworm acceded, and the Spider commenced her task and worked so rapidly that in a short time the web was finished. "Just look at it," she said, "and see how grand and delicate it is. You cannot but acknowledge that I'm a much better worker than you. See how quickly I perform my labors." "Yes," answered the Silkworm, "but hush up, for you bother me. Your labors are designed only as base traps, and are destroyed whenever they are seen, and brushed away as useless dirt; while mine are stored away, as ornaments of Royalty."

True art is thoughtful, delights and endures.

THE FOX AND THE GOAT

By an unlucky chance a Fox fell into a deep well from which he could not get out. A Goat passed by shortly afterwards, and asked the Fox what he was doing down there. "Oh, have you not heard?" said the Fox, "there is going to be a great drought, so I jumped down here in order to be sure to have water by me. Why don't you come down, too?" The Goat thought well of this advice, and jumped down into the well. But the Fox immediately jumped on her back, and by putting his foot on her long horns managed to jump up to the edge of the well. "Good-bye, friend," said the Fox, "remember next time,

Never trust the advice of
a man in difficulties.

THE TWO FELLOWS AND THE BEAR

wo fellows were traveling together through a wood, when a Bear rushed out upon them. One of the travelers happened to be in front, and he seized hold of the branch of a tree, and hid himself among the leaves. The other, seeing no help for it, threw himself flat down upon the ground, with his face in the dust. The Bear, coming up to him, put his muzzle close to his ear, and sniffed and sniffed. But at last with a growl he shook his head and slouched off, for bears will not touch dead meat. Then the fellow in the tree came down to his comrade, and, laughing, said: "What was it that Master Bruin whispered to you?"

"He told me," said the other,

Never trust a friend who
deserts you in a pinch.

THE ROSE AND THE AMARANTH

Rose and an Amaranth blossomed side by side in a garden, and the Amaranth said to her neighbor, "How I envy you your beauty and your sweet scent! No wonder you are such a universal favorite." But the Rose replied with a shade of sadness in her voice, "Ah, my dear friend, I bloom but for a time: my petals soon wither and fall, and then I die. But your flowers never fade, even if they are cut; for they are everlasting."

Greatness carries its own penalties.

THE CAGE BIRD AND THE BAT

A singing bird was confined in a cage which hung outside a window, and had a way of singing at night when all other birds were asleep. One night a Bat came and clung to the bars of the cage, and asked the Bird why she was silent by day and sang only at night. "I have a very good reason for doing so," said the Bird. "It was once when I was singing in the daytime that a fowler was attracted by my voice, and set his nets for me and caught me. Since then I have never sung except by night." But the Bat replied, "It is no use your doing that now when you are a prisoner: if only you had done so before you were caught, you might still have been free."

Precautions are useless after the crisis.

HERCULES AND THE WAGONER

A wagoner was once driving a heavy load along a very muddy way. At last he came to a part of the road where the wheels sank halfway into the mire, and the more the horses pulled, the deeper sank the wheels. So the Wagoner threw down his whip, and knelt down and prayed to Hercules the Strong. "O Hercules, help me in this my hour of distress," quoth he. But Hercules appeared to him, and said:

"Tut, man, don't sprawl there. Get up and put your shoulder to the wheel."

The gods help those who help themselves.

THE DOG AND THE SHADOW

t happened that a Dog had got a piece of meat and was carrying it home in his mouth to eat it in peace. Now on his way home he had to cross a plank lying across a running brook. As he crossed, he looked down and saw his own shadow reflected in the water beneath. Thinking it was another dog with another piece of meat, he made up his mind to have that also. So he made a snap at the shadow in the water, but as he opened his mouth the piece of meat fell out, dropped into the water and was never seen again.

Beware of losing the substance
by grasping at the shadow.

THE ANT AND THE GRASSHOPPER

On a field one summer's day a Grasshopper was hopping about, chirping and singing to its heart's content. An Ant passed by, bearing along with great toil a kernel of corn he was taking to the nest.

"Why not come and chat with me," said the Grasshopper, "instead of toiling and moiling in that way?"

"I am helping to lay up food for the winter," said the Ant, "and recommend you to do the same."

"Why bother about winter?" said the Grasshopper; "we have got plenty of food at present." But the Ant went on its way and continued its toil. When the winter came the Grasshopper had no food, and found itself dying of hunger, while it saw the ants distributing every day corn and grain from the stores they had collected in the summer. Then the Grasshopper knew:

It is best to prepare for the days of necessity.

THE MILKMAID AND HER PAIL

 farmer's daughter had been out to milk the cows, and was returning to the dairy carrying her pail of milk upon her head. As she walked along, she fell amusing after this fashion: "The milk in this pail will provide me with cream, which I will make into butter and take to market to sell. With the money I will buy a number of eggs, and these, when hatched, will produce chickens, and by and by I shall have quite a large poultry-yard. Then I shall sell some of my fowls, and with the money which they will bring in I will buy myself a new gown, which I shall wear when I go to the fair; and all the young fellows will admire it, and come and make love to me, but I shall toss my head and have nothing to say to them." Forgetting all about the pail, and suiting the action to the word, she tossed her head. Down went the pail, all the milk was spilled, and all her fine castles in the air vanished in a moment!

Do not count your chickens
before they are hatched.

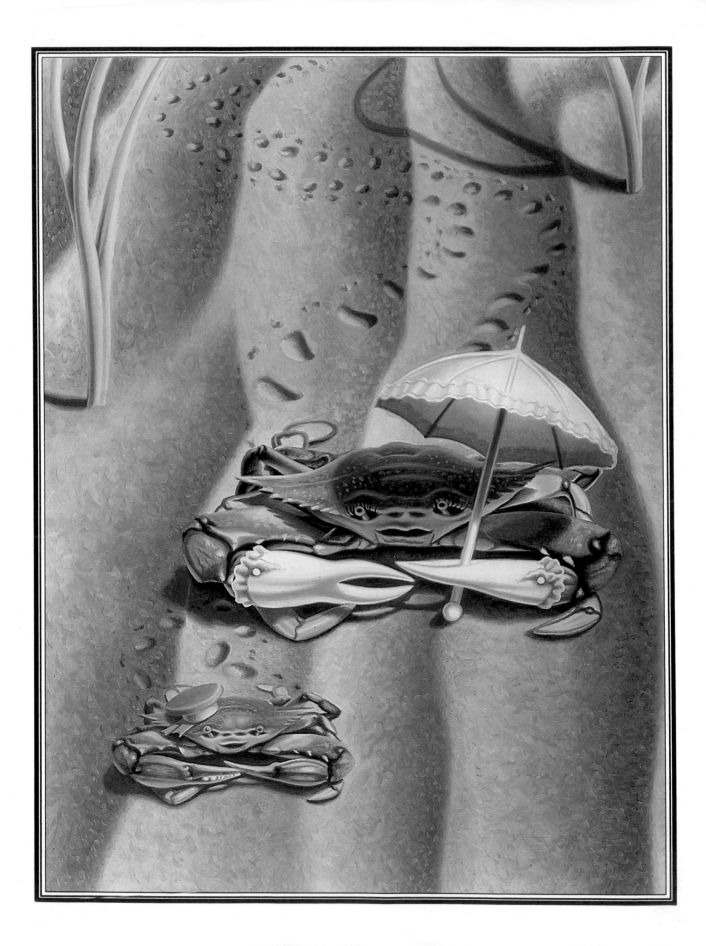

THE TWO CRABS

ne fine day two Crabs came out from their home to take a stroll on the sand. "Child," said the mother, "you are walking very ungracefully. You should accustom yourself to walking straight forward without twisting from side to side."

"Pray, mother," said the young one, "do but set the example yourself, and I will follow you."

Example is the best guidance.

THE TOWN MOUSE AND THE COUNTRY MOUSE

ow you must know that a Town Mouse once upon a time went on a visit to his cousin in the country. He was rough and ready, this cousin, but he loved his town friend and made him heartily welcome. Beans and bacon, cheese and bread, were all he had to offer, but he offered them freely. The Town Mouse rather turned up his long nose at this country fare, and said, "I cannot understand, Cousin, how you can put up with such poor food as this, but, of course, you cannot expect anything better in the country. Come you with me and I will show you how to live. When you have been in town a week, you will wonder how you could ever have stood a country life." No sooner said than done: the two mice set off for the town and arrived at the Town Mouse's residence late at night. "You will want some refreshment after our long journey," said the polite Town Mouse, and took his friend into the grand dining room. There they found the remains of a fine feast, and soon the two mice were eating up jellies and cakes and all that was nice. Suddenly they heard growling and barking. "What is that?" said the Country Mouse. "It is only the dogs of the house," answered the other. "Only!" said the Country Mouse. "I do not like that music at my dinner." Just at that moment the door flew open, in came two huge mastiffs, and the two mice had to scamper down and run off. "Good-bye, Cousin," said the Country Mouse. "What! going so soon?" said the other. "Yes," he replied;

Better beans and bacon in peace,
than cakes and ale in fear.

THE NORTH WIND AND THE SUN

A dispute arose between the North Wind and the Sun, each claiming that he was stronger than the other. At last they agreed to try their powers upon a traveler to see which could soonest strip him of his cloak. The North Wind had the first try. Gathering up all his force for the attack, he came whirling furiously down upon the man, and caught up his cloak as though he would wrest it from him by one single effort: but the harder he blew, the more closely the man wrapped it round himself. Then came the turn of the Sun. At first he beamed gently upon the traveler, who soon unclasped his cloak and walked on with it hanging loosely about his shoulders, then he shone forth in his full strength, and the man, before he had gone many steps, was glad to throw his cloak right off and complete his journey more lightly clad.

Persuasion is better than force.

THE OLD MAN AND DEATH

very poor old man, footsore and bent with years, threw down the heavy bundle of firewood under which he had been groaning, and with tears in his eyes exclaimed: "Oh, hard luck! What pleasure have I ever known? Nothing but work all day—no money—no one to care for me. Alas! I'd sooner Death would take me away." Behold, the grim King of Kings stood before him, dreadful and awe-inspiring, as he rested on his scythe. "Beg pardon, but did I receive a hurry call?" The old man turned all colors and trembling like a leaf, replied, "Please, sir, would you kindly help me to lift this bundle of sticks on to my shoulder?"

We would often be sorry if
our wishes were granted.

MERCURY AND THE WOODMAN

A Woodman was felling a tree on the bank of a river, when his axe, glancing off the trunk, flew out of his hands and fell into the water. As he stood by the water's edge lamenting his loss, Mercury appeared and asked him the reason for his grief. On learning what had happened, out of pity for his distress, Mercury dived into the river and, bringing up a golden axe, asked him if that was the one he had lost. The Woodman replied that it was not, and Mercury then dived a second time, and, bringing up a silver axe, asked if that was his. "No, that is not mine either," said the Woodman. Once more Mercury dived into the river, and brought up the missing axe. The Woodman was overjoyed at recovering his property, and thanked his benefactor warmly; and the latter was so pleased with his honesty that he made him a present of the other two axes. When the Woodman told the story to his companions, one of these was filled with envy of his good fortune and determined to try his luck for himself. So he went and began to fell a tree at the edge of the river, and presently contrived to let his axe drop into the water. Mercury appeared as before, and, on learning that his axe had fallen in, he dived and brought up a golden axe, as he had done on the previous occasion. Without waiting to be asked whether it was his or not, the fellow cried, "That's mine, that's mine," and stretched out his hand eagerly for the prize: but Mercury was so disgusted at his dishonesty that he not only declined to give him the golden axe, but also refused to recover for him the one he had let fall into the stream.

Honesty is the best policy.

THE FOX AND THE MASK

fox had by some means got into the store-room of a theatre. Suddenly he observed a face glaring down on him, and began to be very frightened; but looking more closely he found it was only a Mask, such as actors use to put over their face. "Ah," said the Fox, "you look very fine; it is a pity you have not got any brains."

Outside show is a poor substitute
for inner worth.

THE CROW AND THE PITCHER

A Crow, half-dead with thirst, came upon a Pitcher which had once been full of water; but when the Crow put its beak into the mouth of the Pitcher he found that only very little water was left in it, and that he could not reach far enough down to get at it. He tried, and he tried, but at last had to give up in despair. Then a thought came to him, and he took a pebble and dropped it into the Pitcher. Then he took another pebble and dropped it into the Pitcher. Then he took another pebble and dropped that into the Pitcher. Then he took another pebble and dropped that into the Pitcher. Then he took another pebble and dropped that into the Pitcher. Then he took another pebble and dropped that into the Pitcher. At last, at last, he saw the water mount up near him; and after casting in a few more pebbles he was able to quench his thirst and save his life.

Necessity is the mother of invention.

THE LITTLE BOY AND FORTUNE

 little boy wearied with a long journey, lay down overcome with fatigue on the very brink of a deep well. Being within an inch of falling into the water, Dame Fortune, it is said, appeared to him, and waking him from his slumber, thus addressed him: "Little boy, pray wake up: for had you fallen into the well, the blame will be thrown on me, and I shall get an ill name among mortals; for I find that men are sure to blame their calamities to me, however much by their own folly they have really brought them on themselves."

Every one is more or less master
of his own fate.

THE ASS AND HIS PURCHASER

A man who wanted to buy an Ass went to market, and, coming across a likely-looking beast, arranged with the owner that he should be allowed to take him home on trial to see what he was like. When he reached home, he put him into his stable along with the other asses. The newcomer took a look round, and immediately went and chose a place next to the laziest and greediest beast in the stable. When the master saw this he put a halter on him at once, and led him off and handed him over to his owner again. The latter was a good deal surprised to seem him back so soon, and said, "Why, do you mean to say you have tested him already?" "I don't want to put him through any more tests," replied the other. "I could see what sort of beast he is from the companion he chose for himself."

A man is known by the company he keeps.

THE SHIPWRECKED IMPOSTOR

The shipwrecked Chimpanzee had been clinging for a long time to a slender spar, when a Dolphin came up and offered to carry him ashore. This kind proposition was immediately accepted, and, as they moved along, the Chimp commenced to tell the Fish many marvelous tales, every one of them a bundle of falsehoods. "Well, well, you are indeed an educated chap," said the Dolphin in admiration. "My schooling has been sadly neglected, as I went to sea when but a week old." Just then they entered a large bay, and the Dolphin, referring to it, said, "I suppose you know Herring Roads?" The chimp, taking this for the name of a fellow, and not wishing to appear ignorant, replied: "Do I know Rhodes? Well, I should almost think so! He's an old college chum of mine, and related to our family by—" This was too much for the Dolphin, who immediately made a great leap, and then diving quickly, left the impostor in the air for an instant before he splashed back and disappeared.

A liar deceives no one but himself.

THE ANT AND THE CHRYSALIS

n Ant nimbly running about in the sunshine in search of food came across a Chrysalis that was very near its time of change. The Chrysalis moved its tail, and thus attracted the attention of the Ant, who then saw for the first time that it was alive. "Poor, pitiable animal!" cried the Ant disdainfully. "What a sad fate is yours! While I can run hither and thither, at my pleasure, and, if I wish, ascend the tallest tree, you lie imprisoned here in your shell, with power only to move a joint or two of your scaly tail." The Chrysalis heard all this, but did not try to make any reply. A few days after, when the Ant passed that way again, nothing but the shell remained. Wondering what had become of its contents, he felt himself suddenly shaded and fanned by the gorgeous wings of a beautiful Butterfly. "Behold in me," said the Butterfly, "your much-pitied friend! Boast now of your powers to run and climb as long as you can get me to listen." So saying, the Butterfly rose in the air, and, borne along and aloft on the summer breeze, was soon lost to the sight of the Ant forever.

Appearances are deceptive.

THE SHEPHERD BOY

here was once a young Shepherd Boy who tended his sheep at the foot of a mountain near a dark forest. It was rather lonely for him all day, so he thought upon a plan by which he could get a little company and some excitement. He rushed down towards the village calling out "Wolf, Wolf," and the villagers came out to meet him, and some of them stopped with him for a considerable time. This pleased the boy so much that a few days afterwards he tried the same trick, and again the villagers came to his help. But shortly after this a Wolf actually did come out from the forest, and began to worry the sheep, and the boy, of course, cried out "Wolf, Wolf," still louder than before. But this time the villagers, who had been fooled twice before, thought the boy was again deceiving them, and nobody stirred to come to his help. So the Wolf made a good meal off the boy's flock, and when the boy complained, the wise man of the village said:

A liar will not be believed, even when
he speaks the truth.

THE VIXEN AND THE LIONESS

A Vixen who was taking her babies out for an airing one balmy morning, came across a Lioness, with her cub in arms. "Why such airs, haughty dame, over one solitary cub?" sneered the Vixen. "Look at my healthy and numerous litter here, and imagine, if you are able, how a proud mother should feel." The Lioness gave her a squelching look, and lifting up her nose, walked away, saying calmly, "Yes, just look at that beautiful collection. What are they? Foxes! I've only one, but remember, that one is a Lion."

Quality is better than quantity.

THE HARE AND THE TORTOISE

The Hare, one day, laughing at the Tortoise for his slowness and general unwieldiness, was challenged by the latter to run a race. The Hare, looking on the whole affair as a great joke, consented, and the Fox was selected to act as umpire and hold the stakes. The rivals started, and the Hare, of course, soon left the Tortoise far behind. Having come midway to the goal, she began to play about, nibble the young herbage, and amuse herself in many ways. The day being warm, she even thought she would take a little nap in a shady spot, as, if the Tortoise should pass her while she slept, she could easily overtake him again before he reached the end. The Tortoise meanwhile plodded on, unwavering and unresting, straight toward the goal. The Hare, having overslept herself, started up from her nap, and was surprised to find that the Tortoise was nowhere in sight. Off she went at full speed, but on reaching the winning-post found that the Tortoise was already there, waiting for her arrival.

Slow and steady wins the race.

ABOUT THE ILLUSTRATOR

Walt Sturrock was born in Jersey City, NJ, in 1961. Influenced by Eric Sloane and Maxfield Parrish, he began developing his artistic talents at an early age. After high school, he was awarded scholarships from the Society of Illustrators and the New Jersey Art Director's Club. He earned his Bachelor of Fine Arts degree in illustration from Montclair State College. He then began his freelance career, working in advertising, magazine, and book illustration. His work has been shown in a number of galleries on the east coast. *Aesop's Fables* is Walt's second book for Unicorn Publishing, his first being a limited edition of *A Christmas Carol*. He is looking forward to illustrating many Unicorn classics in the future.